D1570746

To: *Katie*

From: *Virginia* ♡

THE OLD FARMER'S ALMANAC

The Gift of
Gardening

Dedication

May everyone enjoy the beauty, bounty, and inspiration of a garden every day.
—Best wishes from the Almanac and Sellers Publishing editors

Published by Sellers Publishing, Inc.
161 John Roberts Road, South Portland, ME 04106
Visit us at www.sellerspublishing.com • E-mail: rsp@rsvp.com

Copyright © 2018 Sellers Publishing, Inc.
Illustrations © 2018 Kristin Kest
Factoids © Yankee Publishing Incorporated
Managing Editor: Mary L. Baldwin
Production Editor: Charlotte Cromwell
Cover and Interior Design: Mary L. Baldwin, Charlotte Cromwell
Editorial assistance, The Old Farmer's Almanac: Sarah Perreault

ISBN-13: 978-1-4162-4645-9

Printed and bound in China.

10 9 8 7 6 5 4 3 2 1

THE OLD FARMER'S ALMANAC

The Gift of
Gardening

SELLERS

PUBLISHING

Life begins the day
you start a garden.

–Chinese Proverb

The glory of gardening:
hands in the dirt, head in the sun,
heart with nature.
To nurture a garden is to feed not
just the body, but the soul.

-Alfred Austin

*According to Greek tradition, a cactus placed by
the front door will guard a home against evil.*

Learn to be an observer in all seasons. Every single day, your garden has something new and wonderful to show you.

–Author Unknown

I've always felt that having a garden is like having a good and loyal friend.

-C. Z. Guest

For longer-lasting blooms, pick flowers in the late afternoon.

My garden is my
most beautiful
masterpiece.

–Claude Monet

Gardening is the art that uses
flowers and plants as paint
and the soil and sky as canvas.

–Elizabeth Murray

Brighten your garden with native Mexican plants
such as cosmos, dahlias, marigolds, and zinnias.

Each time a flower blooms,

the world is reminded

that there is beauty in

new beginnings.

–Matshona Dhliwayo

If you wish to make anything
grow, you must understand it,
and understand it in a
very real sense.

–Russell Page

When tended the right way,
beauty multiplies.

–Shannon Wiersbitzky

Bury seaweed in garden soil: Root crops will love it.

A garden is a grand teacher.
It teaches patience and
careful watchfulness;
it teaches industry and thrift;
above all it teaches entire trust.

-Gertrude Jekyll

"Primrose" comes from the Middle English word primrose, *meaning "first rose."*

The garden suggests
there might be a place
where we can meet
nature halfway.

–Michael Pollan

Common mud is still the best remedy for bee or wasp stings.

If you have a garden
and a library,
you have everything
you need.

–Cicero

Garden as though you will live forever.

–William Kent

If bees stay at home, rain will soon come; if they fly away, fine will be the day.

Where flowers bloom, so does hope.

-Lady Bird Johnson

Folklore says that the wider the black bands on a woolly bear caterpillar, the harsher the coming winter.

Show me your garden
and I shall tell you
what you are.

-Alfred Austin

Butterflies
are self-propelled
flowers.

–R. A. Heinlein

To attract butterflies, plant brightly colored asters, coneflowers, and verbena.

We come from the earth.
We return to the earth.
And in between we garden.

–Author Unknown

A garden must combine
the poetic and the mysterious
with a feeling of
serenity and joy.

–Luis Barragán

A slice of lemon will clean berry-stained fingers.

Gardening simply does not allow one to be mentally old, because too many hopes and dreams are yet to be realized.

-Allan Armitage

Everything that slows us down and forces patience, everything that sets us back into the slow circles of nature, is a help. Gardening is an instrument of grace.

-May Sarton

To forget how to dig the earth and tend the soil is to forget ourselves.

-Mahatma Gandhi

The first carrots were purple, white, or yellow—not orange!

Why try to explain miracles to your kids when you can just have them plant a garden.

–Robert Brault

Red currant tomatoes contain 40 times more lycopene than domestic tomatoes. This antioxidant helps to prevent heart and kidney disease.

She who plants a garden plants happiness.

–Author Unknown

Use basil as a mosquito repellent by crushing a few leaves and rubbing them onto your skin.

Half the interest of the garden is the constant exercise of the imagination.

–Alice Morse Earle

Blueberries help to slow aging.

It was such a pleasure to sink one's hands into the warm earth, to feel at one's fingertips the possibilities of the new season.

-Kate Morton

Plant lettuce, peas, and spinach when lilacs show their first leaves.

Always do your best.
What you plant now,
you will harvest later.

–Og Mandino

Folklore says that if a girl finds nine peas in a pod,
the next bachelor she meets will become her husband.

Gardening is cheaper than therapy and you get tomatoes.

-Author Unknown

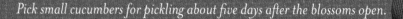

Pick small cucumbers for pickling about five days after the blossoms open.

Let us come alive to the
splendor that is all around us,
and see the beauty
in ordinary things.

–Thomas Merton

If you've never experienced
the joy of accomplishing
more than you can imagine,
plant a garden.

–Robert Brault

"Tulip" probably came from a Turkish word for
"turban," a reference to the flower's shape.

Life began

in a

garden.

–Author Unknown

Ladybugs come in a wide variety of colors, including red, orange, pink, yellow, gray, brown, and black.